LET'S PLAY
I SPY
VEHICLES
Activity Book for kids

YOU WILL FIND INSIDE THIS BOOK DIFFERENT TYPE OF VEHICLES AND THE LETTERS ARE NOT IN THE ALPHABETICAL ORDER.

EDUCATION Fun Books

I SPY WITH MY LITTLE EYE SOMETHING BEGINNING WITH...

C

IS FOR

CAR

I SPY WITH MY LITTLE EYE
SOMETHING BEGINNING WITH...

A
IS FOR
AiRPLANE

I SPY WITH MY LITTLE EYE SOMETHING BEGINNING WITH...

H

IS FOR

HELICOPTER

I SPY WITH MY LITTLE EYE SOMETHING BEGINNING WITH...

B

IS FOR

BICYCLE

I SPY WITH MY LITTLE EYE
SOMETHING BEGINNING WITH...

T

IS FOR

TAXI

I SPY WITH MY LITTLE EYE SOMETHING BEGINNING WITH...

M

IS FOR

MOTORCYCLE

I SPY WITH MY LITTLE EYE SOMETHING BEGINNING WITH...

P

IS FOR

POLICE CAR

I SPY WITH MY LITTLE EYE SOMETHING BEGINNING WITH...

S

IS FOR

SKATEBOARD

I SPY WITH MY LITTLE EYE SOMETHING BEGINNING WITH...

T

IS FOR

TRAIN

I SPY WITH MY LITTLE EYE SOMETHING BEGINNING WITH...

F

IS FOR

FIRE ENGINE

I SPY WITH MY LITTLE EYE SOMETHING BEGINNING WITH...

C

IS FOR

CARRIAGE

I SPY WITH MY LITTLE EYE SOMETHING BEGINNING WITH...

V

IS FOR

VAN

I SPY WITH MY LITTLE EYE SOMETHING BEGINNING WITH...

R

IS FOR

ROWBOAT

I SPY WITH MY LITTLE EYE
SOMETHING BEGINNING WITH...

B

IS FOR

BULLDOZER

I SPY WITH MY LITTLE EYE SOMETHING BEGINNING WITH...

A

IS FOR

AMBULANCE

I SPY WITH MY LITTLE EYE SOMETHING BEGINNING WITH...

D

IS FOR

DUMP TRUCK

I SPY WITH MY LITTLE EYE SOMETHING BEGINNING WITH...

F

IS FOR

FORKLIFT